Pupil Book 4
Composition

Author: Chris Whitney

William Collins' dream of knowledge for all began with the publication of his first book in 1819. A self-educated mill worker, he not only enriched millions of lives, but also founded a flourishing publishing house. Today, staying true to this spirit, Collins books are packed with inspiration, innovation and practical expertise. They place you at the centre of a world of possibility and give you exactly what you need to explore it.

Collins. Freedom to teach.

Published by Collins
An imprint of HarperCollinsPublishers
The News Building
1 London Bridge Street
London
SE1 9GF

Browse the complete Collins catalogue at
www.collins.co.uk

© HarperCollinsPublishers Limited 2015

10 9 8 7 6 5 4 3 2 1

ISBN 978-0-00-813351-1

The author asserts her moral right to be identified as the author of this work.

British Library Cataloguing in Publication Data
A Catalogue record for this publication is available from the British Library

Publishing Manager: Tom Guy
Project Managers: Dawn Booth and Kate Ellis
Edited: Jessica Marshall
Cover design and artwork: Amparo Barrera
Internal design concept: Amparo Barrera
Typesetting: Jouve India Private Ltd
Illustrations: Dante Ginevra, Adrian Bijloo, Aptara and QBS

Printed in Italy by Grafica Veneta S.p.A.

Acknowledgements

The publishers wish to thank the following for permission to reproduce content. Every effort has been made to trace copyright holders and to obtain their permission for the use of copyright materials. The publishers will gladly receive any information enabling them to rectify any error or omission at the first opportunity.

Peters Fraser & Dunlop for an extract from *The Stove Haunting* by Bel Mooney. Reproduced by permission of Peters Fraser & Dunlop (www.petersfraserdunlop.com) on behalf of Bel Mooney; Curtis Brown Group Ltd for an extract from *Alice's Adventures in Wonderland*, dramatised by Clemence Dane, copyright © Clemence Dane, 1948. Reproduced with permission of Curtis Brown Group Ltd, London on behalf of The Beneficiaries of the Estate of Clemence Dane; Celia Warren for the poem "Penguins on Ice" by Celia Warren, from *Wacky Wild Animals*, ed. Brian Moses, Macmillan Childrens Books, 2000, copyright © Celia Warren. Reproduced by kind permission of the author; Scholastic Inc. for the poem "In Praise of Penguins" from *Learn All About Penguins* by Robin Bernard, Scholastic Inc./Teaching Resources, copyright © 1994 by Robin Bernard. Reproduced by permission; HarperCollins Publishers Ltd for an extract from *The Hobbit* by J R R Tolkien, 1991, pp.13-14, copyright © The J R R Tolkien Estate Limited, 1937, 1965. Reproduced by permission of HarperCollins Publishers Ltd; Judith Nicholls for the haiku "Wolf", from *Midnight Forest* by Judith Nicholls, published by Faber & Faber, copyright © Judith Nicholls, 1987. Reproduced by kind permission of the author; and Dr Gervase Phinn for the haiku "Seasonal haiku" by Richard Matthews from *Lizard over Ice*, edited by Gervase Phinn, published by Nelson Thornes Ltd, 1990, copyright © Richard Matthews. Reproduced with kind permission.

(t = top, c = centre, b = bottom)

p. 24 Digital Vision/Getty Images; p. 25 Romolo Tavani/Shutterstock; p. 26 MarcelClemens/Shutterstock; p. 34 iStock/Getty Images; p. 35 (t) iStock/Getty Images; p. 35 (m) Dennis van de Water/Shutterstock; p. 35 (b) George_C/Shutterstock; p. 38 Arsgera/Shutterstock; p. 39 Peter Hodgetts/Alamy; p. 50 Stocktrek Images, Inc./Alamy

MIX
Paper from responsible sources
FSC www.fsc.org   **FSC** C007454

Find out more about HarperCollins and the environment at
www.harpercollins.co.uk/green

Pupil Book 4

Composition

Contents

		Page
Unit 1	Story settings	6
Unit 2	Writing about a character	9
Unit 3	Writing a playscript	13
Unit 4	Writing a realistic story	17
Unit 5	Writing a good ending	20
Unit 6	More story settings	24
Unit 7	Editing	27
Unit 8	Different ways to write a poem	30
Unit 9	Writing haiku	34
Unit 10	Making notes	38
Unit 11	Organising information	41
Unit 12	Writing notes for a newspaper report	45
Unit 13	Writing an explanation	49
Unit 14	Writing an instruction text	53
Unit 15	Writing a letter	57

Story settings

Read the extract from **'The Hobbit'** by **J.R.R. Tolkien**, then answer the questions that follow.

This is an extract from an adventure story. Bilbo Baggins is a hobbit on a journey with a group of dwarfs, seeking treasure. In adventure stories, the characters often have to travel from a safe and comfortable setting into a setting that is grim and dangerous. This extract describes that change in setting.

Use lots of adjectives for an atmospheric description.

Familiar setting

The characters are on a journey so the setting changes.

It sounds a lonely and unwelcoming place.

Personification ('evil' castles seem threatening).

At first, they passed through hobbit-lands, a wide respectable country inhabited by decent folk, with good roads, an inn or two, and now and then a dwarf or a farmer ambling by on business. Then they came to lands where people spoke strangely and sang songs Bilbo had never heard before. Now they had gone on far into the Lone-lands where there were no people left, no inns, and the roads grew steadily worse. Not far ahead were dreary hills, rising higher and higher, dark with trees. On some of them were old castles with an evil look, as if they had been built by wicked people. Everything seemed gloomy, for the weather that day had taken a nasty turn. Mostly it had been as good as May can be, even in merry tales, but now it was cold and wet. In the Lone-lands they had been obliged to camp when they could, but at least it had been dry ...

The weather and the darkness change with the setting, creating atmosphere.

Personification (trees that sigh seem sad and creepy).

Still the dwarves jogged on, never turning round or taking any notice of the hobbit. Somewhere behind the grey clouds the sun must have gone down, for it began to get dark as they went down into a deep valley with a river at the bottom. Wind got up, and willows along its banks bent and sighed. Fortunately the road went over an ancient stone bridge, for the river, swollen with the rains, came rushing down from the hills and mountains in the north.

Get started

Discuss these questions and complete these tasks with a partner.

1. Think of books you have read or that you are reading at the moment. Where are they set?

2. Which settings did you enjoy reading about? Why?

3. Which settings did you not enjoy reading about? Why?

4. Make a list of all the different settings you can think of.

Try these

The setting in the extract changes as Bilbo travels further away from his home. List the words and phrases that describe the hobbit-lands and those that describe the Lone-lands. Then compare the two places.

Hobbit-lands	Lone-lands

Now try these

1. The weather changes on Bilbo's journey, making the atmosphere gloomier the further he travels. The same setting can feel very different depending on the weather. Make a list of what you might see and hear in these settings in good and bad weather. One has been done for you.

Setting	Good weather	Bad weather
A town centre	People in cafes, people wearing sunglasses, shadows on the ground	People with umbrellas, puddles, cars splashing water, miserable people
A rainforest		
Wide open fields		
A beach		

2. Read the extract again and look carefully at the techniques Tolkien uses to create atmosphere. Use your ideas for one of the settings from the previous activity to write two paragraphs showing two different pictures of the same setting.

Writing about a character

Read the extracts from **'The Stove Haunting'** by **Bel Mooney**, then answer the questions that follow.

When you create a character, just telling the reader about them isn't enough. You can also show the reader through what the character says and does, and how the other characters react.

Read this extract from a story set in the early 19th century. Farm workers were very poor. Some villagers in Winterstoke have been holding secret meetings to protest against low pay. One of these villagers is Thomas Leggat, but Daniel, a kitchen boy, discovers that Thomas is a spy.

How characters react to each other tells the reader a lot about them.

There on the path stood Squire Plumtree himself, in his high polished boots and starched white neckcloth, talking to a man who wore the rough clothes of a labourer. Daniel recognised him at once – it was Thomas Leggat, one of the men whom Daniel had seen at the secret ceremony. Why would the Squire stand talking secretly in the cold darkness to a mere farm worker unless …? Daniel started to shiver.

This simile compares Leggat to a trapped animal, making him seem desperate and dangerous.

All characters need a motivation (the reason why they act the way they do). The Squire is paying Leggat to spy, so Leggat's motivation is money.

The man glanced round nervously as he spoke, his eyes glinting in the light from the window like those of an animal at bay. The Squire had a peculiar look of pleasure on his face – not the kind that comes from happiness, but the kind which stems from black, grim satisfaction, as when an opponent has been defeated. Daniel strained his ears to hear. "… and so it is all arranged, and I suggest to you that you keep yourself indoors," the Squire was saying.

"Aye, master," mumbled Leggat.

"That will be all then … Oh, and here's payment for you. "

At that moment – he could not help it – Daniel sneezed.

Both men whirled round.

"Who's hiding there, in the name of God?" called the Squire in a furious voice.

Daniel stepped forward into the light. "It's only me, your worship, with a letter from my master."

Daniel knows there is another secret meeting tonight and he wants to warn the others that Squire Plumtree knows about it.

Just as he reached the gates, however, a figure stepped out from the deeper blackness which encircled them, a figure that had been hiding in the thick bushes by the Manor entrance. It was a man – a tall man who reached

out a strong, bony hand which gripped Daniel painfully by the neck.

He wriggled but the grip tightened – viciously. And then a rough voice growled, "Now my young master, my little listener, I be wanting you to tell me where you're rushing off to, like." The tone was low and menacing, and as Daniel recognised it, his knees seemed to turn to water. It was Thomas Leggat – the man he now knew to be a spy.

Get started

Discuss these questions with a partner.

1. Which character or characters in the extract do you dislike?

2. Why do you feel the way you do about them? Look for evidence in the text.

3. Do you feel the same way about Daniel? Why?

Try these

Find the descriptions in the extract that tell the reader about Squire Plumtree and Thomas Leggat. The descriptions may be telling the reader something about their appearance or about their actions. Decide which and write them under the correct heading.

Name	Their appearance	Their actions
The Squire		
Leggat		

Now try these

1. Write a description of each character in this extract. Try to describe their personalities and what their actions tell us about them, as well as what they look like.

   a) The Squire

   b) Leggat

   c) Daniel

2. Read the last two paragraphs again where Daniel is on his way to the secret meeting to warn others. Rewrite this event from the point of view of Daniel (1st person) and in the past tense. Include details about what Daniel thought and felt as Thomas Leggat held him, as well as describing what he did.

Writing a playscript

Read the playscript adapted from **'Alice's Adventures in Wonderland'** and dramatised by **Clemence Dane**, then answer the questions that follow.

Here is a playscript from a famous story. A playscript is the written instructions for a play (which is a performance of a story). A playscript should have everything the performers need to know to perform the story (what each character says and does, and descriptions of the settings). Because playscripts tell the performers what to say and do, everything is written in the third person and the present tense.

Alice has fallen down a rabbit hole into a very strange sort of place. She has met some very odd characters and, at this point in the play, seems to be lost.

A new scene starts whenever the play changes time or place. This scene is the fifth scene in the play and takes place in a wood.

Spoken words are called 'dialogue'.

Scene 5: In a wood

Cheshire Cat: Miaw!

(Alice looks up. The Cheshire Cat is on a branch above her.)

Alice: Cheshire Puss!

(The Cheshire Cat grins. Alice crosses to the left of the Cheshire Cat.)

Would you tell me please which way I ought to go from here?

Cheshire Cat: That depends on where you want to go.

Alice: I don't care where ...

Cheshire Cat: Then it doesn't matter which way you go.

Alice: What sort of people live about here?

Cheshire Cat: In one direction lives a Hatter, and in the other direction a March Hare. Visit either you like: they're both mad.

Alice: But I don't want to go among mad people.

Cheshire Cat: Oh, we're all mad here. You're mad. I'm mad.

Alice: How do you know that you're mad?

Cheshire Cat: To begin with, a dog's not mad. You grant that?

Alice: I suppose so.

Cheshire Cat: Well then, you see, a dog growls when it's angry and wags its tail when it's pleased. Now I growl when I'm pleased and wag my tail when I'm angry.

Alice: I call it purring, not growling.

Cheshire Cat: Call it what you like! Do you play croquet with the Queen today?

Alice: I haven't been invited yet.

Cheshire Cat: You'll see me there.

(The Cat vanishes.)

Get started

Discuss these questions with a partner.

1. Have you ever been to the theatre?

2. Has a theatre company ever come to your school to perform a play?

3. Have you ever read a play or acted in one?

4. Look at the playscript. How is the playscript different from a storybook?

Try these

Answer these questions and complete these tasks.

1. What do the names followed by colons tell the reader?

2. What is the technical name for the spoken words in a play?

3. What are stage directions for?

4. Why are stage directions in brackets?

5. In your own words, write a definition of a playscript.

6. Write a set of rules to follow for writing a playscript.

Now try these

1. Remember a conversation you've had recently or make one up. Answer these questions about the conversation.

a) What was it about?

b) Who was it with?

c) Where did it happen?

d) When did it happen?

e) Exactly what was said (as best you can remember)?

f) What did you and the other person (or people) do?

2. Write the conversation from question 1 as a full playscript. Include stage directions describing people's actions. Use this checklist to make sure you are writing the playscript correctly.

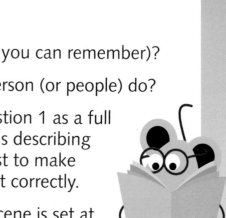

- Write the details of where the scene is set at the beginning.

- Don't use speech marks to show who is speaking.

- Write the speaker's name followed by a colon to show who speaks each line.

- Start a new line each time a character starts to speak.

- Write stage directions to tell the performers what to do.

- Write the stage directions in the third person and the present tense.

- Put the stage directions in brackets.

Writing a realistic story

Read the extract from **'Secret Friends'** by **Elizabeth Laird** then answer the questions that follow.

A realistic story is a piece of fiction set in the real world. The story is made-up but it has believable characters and dialogue, a real-world setting, and events that are possible in real life. It hasn't actually happened, but it could have happened. Realistic stories also deal with problems and issues that affect real people (like this story, which is about bullying and friendship).

> This is likely vocabulary for the narrator to use and it suits the setting.

> This story has a familiar, realistic setting.

It's crazy, starting a new school. For days you feel so new and lost it's as if you've wandered into a foreign country where you can't speak the language. Then, all of a sudden, everything falls into place and you feel you've been there forever.

The people fall into place too. It doesn't take long to work out who's going to be popular and who's going to be out of it, who's going to get into trouble and who's going to be teacher's pet.

It was obvious, from that very first day, that Rafaella was going to be an outsider, on the edge of everything, not liked. No one actually hurt or even teased her much. They just ignored her and left her out of things.

| The dialogue sounds natural and informal. | "What do you want, Earwig?" a group of girls would say, as Rafaella approached them. |

They would stop their conversation to turn and look at her coldly, and she would blush, as she always did, mumble "Nothing," and turn away.

| Scenes like this could be happening all the time. |

I was in those groups sometimes, trying to talk to Kate and Sophie, the two super-popular girls in the class. And I'd watch Rafaella and think, not like that, you idiot. Smile. Say something cool. Don't show you care.

| There aren't usually obvious heroes or villains in realistic stories. |

Get started

Discuss these questions and complete these tasks with a partner.

1. What do you know about the school and its pupils after you have read this extract? Discuss them with a partner and then write three facts.

2. Does the setting feel familiar? Do the characters feel familiar? Talk about things you recognise and relate to in the extract.

Try these

Answer these questions and complete these tasks.

1. What is the definition of a realistic story?
2. Where is this story set?
3. Is the setting a realistic setting? Why?
4. Who are the main characters?
5. Are the main characters believable? Why?
6. What themes are introduced in the extract?
7. Are these themes suitable for a realistic story? Why?
8. Find examples of realistic vocabulary and write them down.

Now try these

1. Have you, or someone you know, ever lost anything? Losing something is a popular theme for a realistic story. Plan your own realistic story by copying and filling in the story plan.

The thing, person or animal that is lost:		
Story title:		
Setting:		
Characters:		
Themes and issues:		
Beginning:	Middle:	End:

2. Read the extract again and look carefully at the annotations that explain the features of a realistic story. Write a scene from your realistic story based on the ideas in your story plan. Include some realistic dialogue between some of the characters you've planned

Writing a good ending

Read the three possible story endings then answer the questions that follow.

At the end of a story, the problems characters have faced are resolved (for better or worse) and then any loose ends are tied up. If you haven't planned this stage you might find yourself inventing messy or silly solutions just to make things tie up.

The story so far: Paul, Mandy and Ali are the last to leave the classroom at playtime. When everyone comes back in, Kate's lunchbox is missing. The teacher questions the three children and, although Paul has taken the lunchbox, all three of them say they know nothing about it. They are sent to the Headteacher.

This is an unhappy ending.

Ali has been blamed incorrectly. Wrong has been followed by more wrong.

Paul gets away with what he's done, which is frustrating.

A good ending doesn't have to be happy. Sad endings can be great to read about too. But, if they're really good, they might make you cry.

Ending 1

"Well," said the Headteacher. "What can you tell me about Kate's lunchbox?"

"Nothing," said Mandy. "I don't know anything."

"And you, Paul? What do you know about it?"

"I saw Ali take it," said Paul.

"That's not true," shouted Ali. "I left the classroom before you did."

"Well, Ali," said the Headteacher, "If Paul says you took it then that must be right. I shall have to ring your mother."

Ending 2

"Well," said the Headteacher. "What can you tell me about Kate's lunchbox?"

"Nothing," said Mandy. "I don't know anything."

"And you, Paul? What do you know about it?" Paul just stood there, looking at the ground.

"I think Paul took it," said Mandy.

"So do I," said Ali. "He was the last in the classroom."

"Well, Paul? What do you say?"

"It was only a joke. I would have given it back."

"Well, Paul, you must return the lunchbox and you must apologise to Kate. We'll say no more about it this time, but if you are ever involved in anything like this again I will have to tell your parents."

Ending 3

"Come in, all of you," said the Headteacher in a stern voice. "Now I understand that you've all been involved in taking someone's lunchbox."

"No, I wasn't involved," protested Mandy.

"Nor was I," said Ali. "The teacher asked us about it because we were the last in the classroom before playtime."

"I really don't care," said the Headteacher. "As far as I'm concerned you're all to blame and you'll all be punished!"

Get started

Discuss these questions and complete these tasks with your partner.

1. Which ending did you like the best? Why?

2. Which ending did you like the least? Why?

3. Think of stories you have read and describe how they ended.

4. In the endings you've discussed, were all the problems resolved and were the loose ends tied up?

Try these

Answer these questions and complete these tasks.

1. What usually happens at the ends of stories?

2. Why is it important to plan the ending of your story?

3. Does a good story ending always have to be a happy one?

4. Think of a story ending you liked. Write a review about why you liked it. What worked well? How did it make you feel?

5. Think of a story ending you didn't like. Write a review about why you didn't like it? What was bad about it? How did it leave you feeling?

6. Think of one fairytale and write out the ending.

Now try these

1. Write a different ending for the story in the extract. Start with these lines from the extract. Plan some ideas and then write your ending.

   The story so far: Paul, Mandy and Ali are the last to leave the classroom at playtime. When everyone comes back in, Kate's lunchbox is missing.

   - What happens next?

   - How is the problem resolved?

   - Is the lunchbox found? If so, where?

   - Will you give it a sad or a happy ending?

2. Read these problems faced by characters in stories. Choose one of the story plots and write a suitable ending for it.

   - Two friends are stranded on the rocks at the seaside and the tide is coming in.

   - Sam, a small boy, has wandered from his garden and is lost.

   - A family are going on holiday when their car breaks down.

More story settings

Look at this photo and the description that follows it, then answer the questions that follow.

There are lots of different techniques you can use to write really powerful descriptions. This short description of the moonscape in the photograph shows you these techniques.

Preposition (to show where the things are that you describe)

Verb (shows what the things you describe are doing)

Adjective phrase (a group of words, some of which are adjectives, describing something)

Noun (an object or thing – the things you describe)

Across the horizon the dusty, cratered surface of the Moon is silently still and lifeless. Overhead, like a jewel, hangs the brilliantly blue Earth, a fragile oasis of colour in the yawning black void of the sky.

Adjective (describing word)

Adverb (describes the verb – how something is done)

Metaphor (a descriptive comparison that leaves out 'like' or 'as')

Simile (a descriptive comparison using 'like' or 'as')

Get started

Discuss these questions and complete these tasks with a partner.

1. Discuss what you know about the Moon and about space.

2. What do you think the surface of the Moon looks like?

3. What do you imagine it is like to be on the Moon?

4. List as many words as you can to describe the Moon. Use a thesaurus if possible.

Try these

The writer has used different techniques to describe the Moon. Find the words and phrases in the extract and write them next to their technical name.

adjective	
preposition	
verb	
adverb	
simile	

Now try these

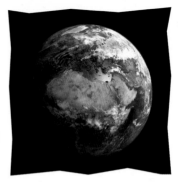

1. The writer describes the Earth as 'like a jewel'. This makes the Earth sound shiny and precious. This is called a simile: using one thing to describe another. Use a simile to describe each of these things. One has been done for you.

   a) He ran as _____ as a _____.

   Answer: *He ran as quickly as a cheetah.*

   b) The stars in the night sky _____ like _____.

   c) The water was as _____ as _____

   d) The night sky was as _____ as _____.

   e) The ice _____ like _____.

   f) The car drove along the street as _____ as _____.

2. A new planet has been discovered. You have been sent to record what you see. In a short paragraph, describe the sight that greets your eyes as you step out of your space vehicle. Using the present tense, use noun phrases and prepositional phrases to describe what you see. Use a simile to make your descriptions more vivid for the reader.

Editing

Read these texts then answer the questions that follow.

Writers have to correct their work to improve it. This shows you some of the things you can do. Look at the corrections that have been made, and then read the edited version.

Don't say the same thing twice.	The astronaut looked around him ~~and looked~~ at the strange world. ~~It was very strange.~~ There was no movement and not a sound could be heard.
Use pronouns instead of repeating nouns.	~~The astronaut~~ᴴᵉ was standing on green rock which glowed. ~~The green rock~~ᴵᵗ stretched as far as he could see.
Add adverbs to show how things are done.	He took a few steps forward. ~~He was cautious~~ᶜᵃᵘᵗⁱᵒᵘˢˡʸ because he did not know what to expect. The ground seemed firm,~~.~~ ~~When he took~~ᵇᵘᵗ ʷⁱᵗʰ his next step he sank into green sand. ~~He sank~~ᴵᵗ ᶜᵃᵐᵉ over his boots and ~~it was hard~~ʰᵉ ˢᵗʳᵘᵍᵍˡᵉᵈ to lift his feet up.
Use conjunctions to join sentences.	
Use precise verbs.	

Edited version

The astronaut looked around him at the strange world. There was no movement and not a sound could be heard.

He was standing on green rock which glowed. It stretched as far as he could see.

He took a few steps forward cautiously because he did not know what to expect. The ground seemed firm, but with his next step he sank into green sand. It came over his boots and he struggled to lift his feet up.

Get started

Look back through your work this year. Discuss these questions and complete these tasks with a partner.

1. Can you find any work where you had to make corrections?

2. What corrections did you make and why?

3. Can you find any errors that still need correcting?

4. Make a note of any errors and corrections you find.

5. Are there any spelling, punctuation or grammar rules you need to revise?

Try these

The writer makes several mistakes in their writing about the astronaut. What can you learn from their mistakes? Make a list of these things as a reminder.

Now try these

1. The extract finishes with the astronaut in danger. Write the next part of the story from where the extract finishes:

   > The ground seemed firm, but with his next step he sank into green sand. It came over his boots and he struggled to lift his feet up.

2. Reread your work and check it for errors using the list you made previously. Check your spelling, punctuation, grammar and vocabulary. Could any of these be improved? If so, make the changes. Use a thesaurus if you need to. When you have edited your work and you are completely happy with it, read it aloud to a partner. Show them your work and ask for feedback. Then do the same for them. Remember to only give constructive criticism.

Different ways to write a poem

Read **'Penguins on Ice'** by **Celia Warren** and **'In Praise of Penguins'** by **Robin Bernard** then answer the questions that follow.

These poems show you how two different poets write about the same topic in their own way.

Penguins on Ice

Three verses, each with four lines.

The rhyme scheme is AABB (the first and second lines rhyme, and the third and fourth lines rhyme).

Each line has four or five syllables.

Each line has four or five syllables.

This is called a refrain (a repeated part of a poem).

Every penguin's mum
Can toboggan on her tum.
She can only do that
As she's fluffy and fat:
    It must be nice
    to live on ice.

Every penguin's dad
Is happy and glad.
He can slip and slide
And swim and glide:
    It must be nice
    to live on ice.

All penguin chicks
Do slippery tricks.
They waddle and fall
But don't mind at all:
    It must be nice
    to live on ice.

In Praise of Penguins

These funny birds in fancy clothes may waddle in the snow,

But when they reach the icy sea
Just watch how fast they go!
Their song sounds like a donkey's bray, they cannot soar or fly,
Yet penguins manage very well, and let me tell you why …
Their feathers keep out water, their blubber keeps out cold,
Their wings make perfect paddles, because they do not fold!
Their tails are good for steering, they brake with both their feet –
So tell me now, from all you've heard …
Aren't penguins NEAT?

One verse made up of nine lines.

These lines together are the same length as the other lines. They could be one line but they have been split, emphasising the rhythm.

Addresses the reader directly: questions and using 'you'.

Most lines are 14 syllables long but these have 13 syllables with a slight pause in the middle that keeps the rhythm going.

This line has an ellipsis (three dots) in the middle, which tells the reader to pause.

Get started

Discuss these questions and complete these tasks with a partner.

1. How does the second poem, 'In Praise of Penguins', describe penguins? Make a list of the words and phrases used to describe penguins.

2. How does the first poem, 'Penguins on Ice', describe penguins? Make a list of descriptive words and phrases from the poem.

3. What similarities and what differences can you find in the descriptions of penguins in the two poems?

Try these

These poems are structured very differently. Copy and complete the table with information about the two poems.

	Penguins on Ice	In Praise of Penguins
Number of verses		
Number of lines per verse		
Number of syllables per line		
Rhyme scheme		
Refrain		

Now try these

1. Think of an animal that you want to write a poem about. Research some facts about your chosen animal. Think of poetic vocabulary you can use to describe it. Then copy and complete the table in order to plan and structure your poem.

This poem is about:
Animal facts and research:
Vocabulary to describe the animal:
Number of verses:
Number of lines per verse:
Number of syllables per line (this can vary but should follow a pattern):
Rhyme scheme (if using one):
Refrain (if including one):

2. Now that you have planned your poem, write it out in full. Try to use some poetic devices such as alliteration, personification, simile or metaphor if you can. Make sure you use plenty of descriptive, poetic language.

Writing haiku

Read these three poems, **'Mark'** by **Helen White**, **'Wolf'** by **Judith Nicholls** and **'Seasonal Haiku'** by **Richard Matthews**, then answer the questions that follow.

Haiku is a Japanese form of poetry and is one of the shortest poetic forms in the world. The point of a haiku is to capture and express a single idea (a moment, a feeling, an object, an animal or a person) in just three lines.

Haiku always follow the same structure. The first line has five syllables.

There are seven syllables in the second line.

Mark

Hair a tangled mop
Broken teeth and runny nose
That's my brother Mark.

There are five syllables in the third line; and seventeen altogether.

The last line should round off or sum up what the poem's all about.

Wolf

still on his lone rock
stares at the uncaged stars and
cries into the night

Haiku don't normally rhyme.

'Wolf' captures a single moment of a wolf howling in the night.

This poem is made up of four haiku, one for each season.

Haiku traditionally describe nature.

Seasonal Haiku

Buds full, fat and green
Pink blossoms trembling on trees
The warm breath of SPRING.

A burnished brass face
In an empty, cloudless sky
Smiles with SUMMER heat.

Curled and twisted leaves
Carpet red the cold dead earth.
AUTUMN'S withered hand.

Bitter winds of ice
Brittle grass like icy spikes
Old soldier WINTER.

Get started

Discuss these questions and complete these tasks with a partner.

1. Read the haiku and discuss the effect each one has. What picture does each haiku paint?

2. Look carefully at 'Seasonal Haiku'. What do you notice about it?

3. Write a sentence for each haiku describing in your own words the picture each haiku paints.

Try these

Use the example haiku and the annotations to answer these questions.

1. Where are haiku from?

2. What is the aim of a haiku?

3. How many lines do haiku have?

4. How many syllables are there in each line of a haiku?

5. Do haiku have a rhyme scheme?

6. What should the last line of a haiku do?

7. What are haiku traditionally about?

Now try these

1. Most haiku traditionally describe something in nature. If you were writing a haiku about the following things, what picture would you want to paint in the reader's mind? Write adjectives and/or noun phrases for each of these haiku topics. One has been done for you.

   a) A winter snowfall

   Answer: *white snowflakes, thick carpet of snow, snowballs*

   b) A forest

   c) A thunderstorm

   d) The night sky

   e) A mountain

2. Choose one of the haiku topics and use your adjectives and noun phrases to write a haiku. Copy and complete the planning grid first, checking you have the correct number of syllables in each line, then write the haiku out in full.

Line	Syllables		Write the line here
1	5		
2	7		
3	5	This should 'sum up' the rest of your haiku.	

Making notes

Read the article about Mount Everest, then answer the questions that follow.

Selecting information and making notes are important skills that writers use all the time. This unit will improve your note-making skills, using this article about Mount Everest to practise on.

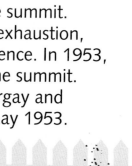

> Mount Everest, at 8840 metres (29 002 feet or about 5.5 miles), is the highest mountain in the world. It is part of a range of very high mountains to the north of India called the Himalaya. These mountains are in Nepal and Tibet. They are so high that they are always covered in snow and ice. There is very little oxygen at these high altitudes, so climbers need to carry supplies of oxygen in tanks on their backs.

The mountain was named after Sir George Everest, who was the first to measure its height in 1849.

In the 1920s and 1930s, many teams of climbers attempted to reach the peak. All of these teams were helped by Sherpa people, who live in the mountains and know them well. They acted as porters, carrying food, tents and tanks of oxygen.

In 1952, a Sherpa called Tenzing Norgay worked with a Swiss expedition that climbed within 200 metres of the summit. This team had to turn back because of cold and exhaustion, but Tenzing learned a great deal from this experience. In 1953, he helped the British team succeed in reaching the summit. The team was led by John Hunt, but Tenzing Norgay and Edmund Hillary were the first at the top on 29 May 1953.

Teams still try to reach the summit today. Sadly, many are killed in the attempt. Some do succeed, though. In 1975, a group of Japanese women made the ascent and one of them, Junko Tabei, was the first woman to reach the summit.

Get started

Discuss these questions and complete these activities with a partner.

1. What is the main topic of this article?

2. Write a sentence describing the main topic in this article.

3. Look at the information in each paragraph and think of a subheading for each one.

Try these

Complete these tasks.

1. Find all the facts in the article about Sherpas and Tenzing Norgay. Write them in a bullet point list.

2. Find all the facts in the article about women climbers. Write them in a bullet point list.

3. Find all the facts in the article about the actual mountain, Mount Everest. Write them in a bullet point list.

4. Use the information in the article to make a timeline from 1849 to 1975.

Now try these

1. Read the whole article again and consider the three titles in the table. Add notes underneath the titles, taking the facts from the article.

Geography	Statistics	Climbers

2. Write a summary of the article describing what the article is about and what types of information is included in it. Try to use no more than 50 words.

Organising information

Read the extract, then answer the questions that follow.

You can make information easy to understand by using headings, lists, bullet points and numbers. Paragraphs can be useful for particular topics or themes.

> The main heading tells the reader what the whole text is about.

> Bullet points are used to clearly separate items in a list.

School Sports Day

Our School Sports Day will be held at Nuffield Primary School on Thursday, 4th July.

Each competitor will try to score points for their house.

We will have three running races for each age group:

- sprint
- skipping race
- egg and spoon race.

There will also be other events for KS2 children:

- high jump
- throwing the bean bag
- long jump
- obstacle race.

The afternoon will finish with running races for parents.

Timetables tell the reader when things are scheduled to happen.

Timetable

1:00	KS1 races
1:30	Y3 and Y4 jumping and throwing events
2:30	Y3 and Y4 races; Y5 and Y6 jumping and throwing events
3:00	Y5 and Y6 races
3:30	Mums' race
3:40	Dads' race

Prizes

There will be a badge and certificate for the first three in each race.

1. The winner of each race will score three points.

2. Second place will score two points.

3. Third place will get one point.

The house that gets most points at the end of the afternoon wins the athletics cup.

Numbered lists should be used when the order of things is important.

Reminders

- Class 6 will be selling orange juice and biscuits, in aid of charity. Remember to bring your money!

- Each class will have an exhibition in the hall of work they have done about their favourite sports.

- Bring your digital camera to get some great shots for the Best Sports Photograph competition!

Subheadings help you to organise your information and help the reader find specific information faster.

Get started

Discuss these questions and complete these tasks with a partner.

1. How has the information in the extract been organised?

2. Make a list of the different organisational features and devices that have been used.

3. Why is it important to organise information?

Try these

Answer these questions about the extract.

1. How has information about the races been organised?

2. Which features tell the reader what each section is about?

3. How are the different event times organised and displayed?

4. Why are the prizes presented in a numbered list?

5. What information is presented in bullet point lists?

6. What information has been presented in a short paragraph?

7. What does the main heading tell the reader?

Now try these

1. Imagine you are organising the end of term class party. Copy and complete the table making notes under each heading.

Title of event	Date and time	Location	List of food to eat	Timetable of events

2. Using your party ideas, design a poster or flyer for your class party. Make sure it has all the information your classmates need to know and that it is organised clearly. Look back at how the information in the extract has been organised and use some or all of the features from the extract: headings and subheadings, bullet point or numbered lists, timetables and short paragraphs.

Writing notes for a newspaper report

Read these notes then answer the questions that follow.

When journalists report on events they make lots of notes.
Here are the notes a reporter made about a hospital fête.
The information in these notes can be organised into paragraphs
and written up in full sentences later.

> Headings help to organise notes.

> Newspaper articles report facts that answer the five questions: who, what, where, when and why?

> Reporters inerview people and quote them in their report.

> 'Hospital fête raises over £3500!' could be the headline. It should sum up the article and grab the reader's attention.

Event:

Caversham Hospital annual summer fête

Weather:

started hot and sunny, not a cloud in the sky until wind and thunder storm came up suddenly

Attendance:

very well attended, hospital grounds full of adults (including nurses and doctors), children and lots of grandparents too!

Purpose:

to collect money for equipment for the children's ward; raised over £3500

Activities:

Army parachute display team – difficult jump because of windy conditions, although all but one parachutist landed on the target. The one who missed finished in the hospital car park with parachute caught on a lamp post.

Mini motorbike racing – nasty crash but doctors and nurses quickly on scene and no serious injuries, though one child taken into the hospital!

Many other stalls and sideshows, including bouncy castle, always a favourite, welly throwing, tombola, wet-sponge throwing at the hospital administrator (seemed lots of the nurses were getting their own back).

Get started

Discuss these questions with a partner.

1. What newspapers do you know of? What is your local paper? Does your school have a paper?

2. Have you ever read a report in a newspaper (paper or online)? If so, what was the story?

3. Have you (or anyone you know) ever been in a newspaper? If so, what was it for?

Try these

Read the reporter's notes about Caversham Hospital annual summer fête and answer the questions.

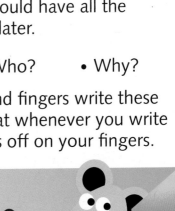

1. What was the event?

2. Who was there?

3. Why was it held?

4. What was the weather like?

5. Does the reporter write in full sentences? Why?

The bullet-point questions below help news reporters to make good notes while they are at the events they write about. If they make notes about all five questions, they should have all the information they need to write a full report later.

- What?   • Where?   • When?   • Who?   • Why?

Draw around your hand. On your thumb and fingers write these five questions. Remember this picture so that whenever you write about an event you can count the questions off on your fingers.

Now try these

1. Think of an event that has happened at your school. It could be an author visit, a school trip, a school play, a class assembly, or any other event that interests you. Copy and complete the table, thinking up a headline and writing notes to answer the questions about your event.
   These questions help news reporters to make good notes about the events they write about. Add a quote about the event from someone who was there. (If you can't get a real one, make one up.)

Headline:
What?
Where?
When?
Who?
Why?
Quote about the event:
Person who gave the quote:

2. Use the notes you made about your school event to write a report about it. Remember to write in full sentences. Add two or three sentences about something that went wrong at your event!

Writing an explanation

Read the report then answer the questions that follow.

This text is an explanation of how a famous disaster happened. The aim of an explanation text is always to answer a question of 'why?' or 'how?' This text answers the question 'How did the "Titanic" sink?'

How the 'Titanic' sank

Explanations are often full of facts and figures.

The passenger liner 'Titanic' was built in Belfast, Northern Ireland, in 1908–1912. She was 269 metres long and weighed 52 310 tons.

On 10 April 1912 she set off from Southampton on her maiden voyage. She carried 2224 passengers and crew. Some of the passengers were very rich, whilst others were fairly poor people going to America to start a new life.

When she was built, 'Titanic' was called 'unsinkable' as she had very modern safety features. However, she didn't have enough lifeboats for all the people on board. There were only enough for 1178 people so, when disaster struck, 1502 people died.

So how did this 'unsinkable' ship sink?

Hull   Compartments

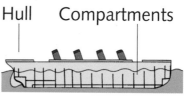

The compartments in the lower part of the ship did not reach the hull. Air could flow from one compartment to another.

These simple drawings are diagrams.

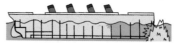

In the foggy waters near Newfoundland, 'Titanic' hit an iceberg that punctured five of her 16 compartments. It happened at 23:40 on 14 April.

Diagrams have to be simple to give information as clearly as possible.

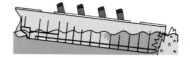

Water filled the punctured compartments, but it also flowed into those that were not damaged.

These diagrams explain, stage-by-stage, why 'Titanic' sank.

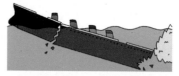

By 2:10 on 15 April, the decks were under water. 'Titanic' broke in two and sank to the bottom of the sea.

This photograph shows the reader what 'Titanic' really looked like.

Get started

Answer these questions and complete these tasks with your partner.

1. What questions would you like the answers to? Make a list.

2. What questions do you already know the answers to? Make a list.

3. Each choose a question you know the answer to.

4. Provide each other with an explanation to your chosen question.

Try these

1. What is the aim of an explanation text?

2. What information do the four diagrams show?

3. What are captions and what is their purpose?

4. What does the photograph show the reader?

5. Write a short summary of the information included in each paragraph.

6. Copy out any technical language the writer has used. Look it up in a dictionary if you need to.

Now try these

1. Think of something you are learning about or that you are interested in. Ask a 'why?' or 'how?' question about it. What diagrams could you use to help explain the answer? What captions or labels would you need? Copy and complete the table in order to plan an explanation text of your own.

Question:
Answer:
Diagrams:
Captions:
Other features (such as headings, labels, lists):
Technical language needed:

2. Using the notes you have made, write your explanation text. Remember, the aim is to answer the question you have chosen, explaining things as clearly as possible to your reader. Share your finished text with your partner and check that they understand your explanation. Then do the same for them.

Writing an instruction text

Read these instructions, then answer the questions that follow.

A set of instructions is a non-fiction text that explains to the reader how to do something. Instructions must be clear and easy to follow. Here are some instructions to make a hovercraft.

Diagrams show the reader what to do in a way that words can't.

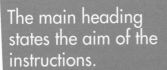

Making a hovercraft

You will need:

scissors

stiff paper

ruler

pencil or pen

paints or colouring pens

sticky tape

balloon

The main heading states the aim of the instructions.

Equipment is listed first so the reader can make sure they have it all before they start.

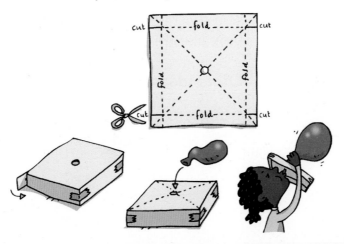

53

Subheadings help to organise the instructions.

The step-by-step instructions are given in a numbered list because their order is important.

Instructions use a lot of imperative (bossy) verbs.

There are nine steps to making this hovercraft.

Instructions for making things need lots of vocabulary of position and placement.

What to do:

1. Cut a piece of paper 12 cm × 12 cm.

2. Measure 2 cm from each of the four sides and draw lines.

3. Find the centre of the paper by drawing two diagonal lines. Where they meet is the centre.

4. In the centre, cut a hole about the size of a 20p coin.

5. Make four short cuts, one on each corner, as shown in the diagram.

6. Colour your hovercraft.

7. Fold in the corners as shown to make a box shape.

8. Use the sticky tape to hold the corners in position.

9. Pull the balloon through the hole and blow it up from underneath.

The finished model should look like this.

Other ideas:

Try making hovercrafts of other shapes and sizes.

Get started

Discuss these questions with a partner.

1. When have you had to follow a set of instructions? What were they for?

2. Have you ever written any instructions before? What were they for?

3. What is the most important thing about instructions?

Try these

Complete the tasks and answer the questions about the instructions for making a hovercraft.

1. What is the aim of these instructions?

2. Why have diagrams been included?

3. Why are the instructions presented in a numbered list?

4. What are imperative verbs?

5. Find all the imperative verbs and make a list.

6. Find examples of positional language and write them down.

Now try these

1. Choose something that you know how to make and write a set of instructions for making it. Only use resources and equipment that are available. Copy and complete the table to help you organise your instructions and to make sure you do not leave anything out. Draw diagrams with the instructions to make things as clear as possible.

Title: Instructions for making a _____	
Equipment:	
Instructions (including diagrams):	
Any additional comments:	

2. Swap instructions with a partner. They follow your instructions and you follow theirs. Gather the resources and the equipment you need.

Then follow each step carefully to the end. Afterwards have completed the instructions, give feedback on how easy the instructions were to follow. Was there anything your partner forgot to include? Your partner should do the same for you.

Writing a letter

Read the letter of complaint, then answer the questions that follow.

When writing a formal letter, you should use formal language and Standard English throughout. How you sign off depends on whether you know the name of the person you're writing to or not. If you know, use 'Yours sincerely'; if you don't, use 'Yours faithfully'. Whether you know the person or not, you can always sign off with 'Yours truly'.

Jenny's address	23 Centre Crescent Upper Blaxland Suffolk XI 2YY
The date Jenny wrote the letter.	Wednesday 4 July 2015
Greeting	Dear Mr Smith,
The structure of the letter is important.	Last week I bought a new bike from your shop. At first I was very pleased with it, but already things have started to go wrong. When I came into the shop to tell you about it, the assistant said that you are on holiday and that I should write a letter.
Jenny explains why she is writing and what she is writing about.	

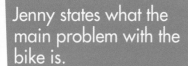

Jenny states what the main problem with the bike is.

A list of other little problems with the bike.

An example of formal language.

The aim is to persuade Mr Smith to put things right.

The worst thing is that Mum and I cannot tighten the saddle, no matter how hard we try. This means that it moves slightly as I am riding along. I think you would agree that this is very dangerous.

There are other problems as well. The bell is stiff and doesn't ring properly, the brakes on the back wheel are rubbing and the left-hand pedal squeaks.

As I had to save for a long time to buy my bike at a rather high price, I'm sure you will agree that these things should be put right.

Yours sincerely,
Jenny Lindman

Get started

Discuss these questions and complete the tasks with a partner.

1. Have you ever written a letter? Have you ever received a letter?

2. Why do people write letters? Think of as many reasons as you can and write them down.

3. Do you think that people mostly write emails now instead of letters? Do the same rules apply?

Try these

Answer the questions and complete the task.

1. What is the aim of Jenny's letter?

2. How does Jenny end her letter?

3. Does Jenny know Mr Smith personally?

4. What sort of language does Jenny use?

5. What has Jenny included in the top right of her letter?

6. Write a summary of each paragraph of Jenny's letter.

Now try these

1. Imagine you have been asked to write a letter of complaint to your local council about one of the following:

   • Parking outside your school, which is endangering children

   • Litter in the streets outside your school

   • No play facilities for children in your local area

Think about what your main argument is and what you would like the council to do about it. Plan your letter under these headings in the table.

Address and date	(Where will this go?)
Formal greeting	(Do you know their name?)
First paragraph	(What has happened to make you write this letter?)
Second paragraph	(What do you want the council to do?)
Signing off	(If you know the person's name, use 'Yours sincerely'; if you don't, use 'Yours faithfully'.)

2. Write your letter of complaint using the planning table to remind you of what to include. This time you should write in full sentences and use formal language.